A Museum Once Forgotten:

REBIRTH OF

The John and Mable

RINGLING

Museum of Art

Copyright © 2007 The John & Mable Ringling Museum of Art
The State Art Museum of Florida
5401 Bay Shore Rd.
Sarasota, FL 34243
www.ringling.org

Copyright © 2007 all photographic material

All rights reserved. No part of this publication may be reproduced
in any manner without prior permission in writing, from
The John & Mable Ringling Museum of Art and other
appropriate copyright holders.

The John & Mable Ringling Museum of Art
5401 Bay Shore Rd.
Sarasota, FL 34243

ISBN 978-0-916758-54-7

Library of Congress Control Number
2006939182

Text by: John Wetenhall, Ph.D.
Project Managed by: Ringling Museum Marketing and Communications
Designed by: Design Marketing Group, Inc.
Printing Partially Underwritten by: Serbin Printing, Inc.

The John and Mable Ringling Museum of Art
    Dr. John Wetenhall, Executive Director
Florida State University
    Dr. Thomas Kent "T.K." Wetherell, President

Contents

Director's Preface: The Extraordinary Transformation

The public dedication of the John M. McKay Visitors Pavilion on February 1, 2007, marks the completion of one of the most extraordinary transformations of any museum in North America. It is a story of riches to ruin, and back again.

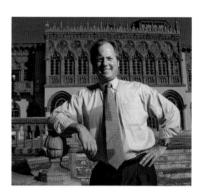

The wonder of the "Ringling Renaissance" lies in the distressingly poor condition into which the Museum had fallen by the late 1990s. The Ringling Mansion, *Cà d'Zan*, had to be closed for a renovation that required $15 million and six years. The building that housed the Historic Asolo Theater was condemned. The Art Museum roof was failing. Seemingly out of desperation, in 2000 governance was transferred from Florida's Department of State to Florida State University (FSU), and – through the forward-looking vision of FSU President Sandy D'Alemberte, our local Board of Directors, and Senate President John McKay – funds were secured to restore the original Ringling buildings and later to construct all four buildings on the Museum's Master Plan: an expansion of our Circus Museum, a Visitors Pavilion, an Education Complex, and Art Galleries. And so within a mere six years, the new partnership between the local community and FSU at once restored the original Ringling Estate and expanded it to provide first-rate facilities for a 21st century museum.

Our other story is financial. John Ringling's estate included $1.2 million for care of the Museum and its collection. When FSU assumed governance 64 years later, the endowment had hardly grown to $2 million – the fault of poor money management combined with little community financial support (State officials believed the Museum to be a community responsibility; local residents thought that Florida should support the "State Art Museum of Florida"). In 2002, when $43 million was provided through the State for new buildings, it came with a condition that our Board of Directors would raise $50 million for endowment within five years. Impossible as the task then seemed, it succeeded. By the project's completion in February 2007, over $56 million has been donated or pledged to endowment, marking the first major commitment to the Ringling's long-term stability since John Ringling's original bequest in 1936.

In all, over $140 million has been invested in the Ringling Museum. Its size has doubled. Its financial stability has been addressed. The Estate has been restored to its original grandeur. The John and Mable Ringling Museum of Art is now one of the 20 largest art museums in North America, and in the years ahead – by refining collections, enhancing exhibitions and establishing first-class programming for audiences of all ages – will strive to become one of the very finest.

John Wetenhall, Ph.D.
Executive Director

> "I hope this museum...will promote education and art appreciation, especially among our young people."
>
> — John Ringling, at the Ringling Museum dedication ceremony in 1931

A Museum Once Forgotten

It begins with an unlikely story. A small town boy from rural Wisconsin joined his brothers to form a traveling show that would grow from the dabbling amusements of show-biz amateurs to one of the grandest spectacles in the history of American entertainment. In an era before television and radio, the "Boys from Baraboo" barnstormed the Midwest, bought out their competitors including "Barnum & Bailey" and branded the "The Greatest Show on Earth." The brothers were master marketers, filling the big tops to capacity. By the 1920s, John Ringling's circus fortune placed him on the cover of *TIME Magazine* as one of the wealthiest men in America. He and his beloved Mable purchased property in Sarasota with hopes of creating a winter paradise, and John acquired large tracks of land along the bay and barrier islands for investment. Sarasota would become their winter home.

The Shangri-La of Circus Dreams – Cà d'Zan

Having traveled often to Europe in search of circus acts, John and Mable came to appreciate the finer pleasures of culture and the exotic treasures of the continent's dazzling architecture. They fell in love with the romance of Venice, and determined that their home on Sarasota Bay would emulate the grandeur of the Doge's Palace, combined with the gothic grace of the Cà d'Oro. Sarasota Bay would become their Grand Canal. In 1924, they commissioned New York architect Dwight James Baum to build their dream, to be known through Venetian dialect as the "House of John," but in reality, what a later writer would christen "his love letter to Mable." The mansion was completed in 1926, and would soon become the epicenter of cultural life on Florida's west coast, attracting such luminaries as New York Mayor Jimmy Walker, entertainer Flo Ziegfeld, comedian Will Rogers, and many others. Lavish parties were held into the morning hours, orchestras serenading guests from the Ringling yacht, moored a few feet off the marble terrace. But it was not to last. Within three years, in 1929, Mable would die of diabetes complicated by Addison's disease.

A Museum Once Forgotten

Florence and Rome in Sarasota – The Museum of Art

European travel had kindled in the Ringlings a passion for art. "Mr. John," as Ringling was known, sought out the advice of savvy art dealers such as Julius Böhler and became a regular at the New York and London auctions. He purchased masterpieces by Rubens, Van Dyck, Titian, Tintoretto, Veronese, Velázquez, El Greco, Tiepolo, Gainsborough and Reynolds. Flush with wealth primarily from the circus, but also from other smart investments in oil, real estate and the railroad, he bought whole rooms, like the Astor Salon and Library from the great New York Astor mansion about to be demolished. He even purchased a collection of Cypriot antiquities from the Metropolitan Museum of Art among other fine works. He dreamed of building his own museum, in the spirit of Morgan and Frick, to transform Sarasota into a cultural destination.

In 1925, Ringling engaged architect John H. Phillips to design a palace for his treasures, a museum that would emulate the footprint of Florence's Uffizi Gallery, echoing its graceful colonnades and opening onto an Italianate garden. Above, heavy balustrades adorned with monumental sculptures would recall Bernini's colonnade around St. Peter's Square at the Vatican in Rome. The renderings even envisioned an addition to one day house a school for artists – a vision that would later become Sarasota's Ringling School of Art and Design separate from the Museum of Art.

Construction began in 1927, but was slowed almost immediately by the collapse of Florida's land boom and later, Wall Street's stock market crash. Financial misfortune and Mable's death might have ended the dream, but "Mr. John" instead gained a new resolve to complete his museum, borrowing money as needed, knowing that it would perpetuate the memory of his beloved Mable. In October 1931, "The John and Mable Ringling Museum of Art" was officially dedicated and opened to the public.

Though the circus continued its travels across North America, the Depression brought John Ringling's fortune to an end, as creditors slowly gathered to tear apart his estate. But ever the shrewd businessman and without children to claim inheritance, Mr. Ringling named the State of Florida as his beneficiary, entrusting his treasures to its people and through governmental liens, keeping his collection intact and the remaining cash beyond the reach of creditors. At his death in 1936, John Ringling bequeathed his entire estate – then 32-acres on Sarasota Bay, *Cà d'Zan*, the Museum of Art, its art masterpieces, and $1.2 million in operating endowment – to the people of Florida, and so preserved in perpetuity The John and Mable Ringling Museum of Art. Some would call this "his greatest triumph."

A Responsibility Shared by None

For nearly ten years, the Ringling Museum was opened irregularly and not professionally maintained. *Cà d'Zan*, was used privately and remained closed to the public, while the State of Florida fought with creditors over the fate of the estate and its artistic treasures. By 1946, the State had prevailed, as title at last transferred to the people of Florida. The Museum opened under the leadership of its first director, A. Everett "Chick" Austin, Jr., who contributed to the Ringling legacy by establishing the Ringling Circus Museum in 1948, and soon thereafter in 1950, purchasing from an Italian art dealer the interior of an 18th-century court theater from Asolo, a hilltop village north of Venice.

Under normal circumstances, the $1.2 million endowment would have grown over time, its proceeds preserving the estate and its treasures. It even might have attracted more donors, creating a basis of wealth to enhance the Museum's collections and further its educational mission. But it did not.

Managed by government, the funds languished without the benefit of strategic investing. Meanwhile the local community, convinced that the Ringling Museum was the State's responsibility, did little to support the Ringling Museum. Gradually, the care that aging buildings require – weatherproofing, mechanical upgrades, and occasional refurbishing – was put off or handled piecemeal. As neglect led to crisis, private supporters came forth to keep the Museum open, while dedicated and under funded staff struggled to fulfill the Museum's vast potential. But over time the challenge became overwhelming.

By the late 1990s, the decay from deferred maintenance had reached a critical point. The *Cà d'Zan* mansion was falling apart, its once gracious terrace and dock unsafe for public occupancy and its interiors hardly resembling the elegance of Mable Ringling's times. The roof of the Museum of Art leaked, threatening the extraordinary works inside and damaging the opulent architecture. The building completed in 1957 to house the Historic Asolo Theater was condemned. Antiquated security systems no longer provided adequate protection for art. Weathered footpaths and cracking roads gave the once venerable estate a tiring look of ruin. *Cà d'Zan* had deteriorated so badly by the mid-1990s that it had to be closed for restoration, but not before one final indignity: it served as the centerpiece for the 1996 remake of Dickens' epic novel, *Great Expectations* – as Miss Havisham's decrepit ruin.

Timeline

1936 Upon his death, John Ringling bequeathed his estate to the State of Florida.

1946 The John and Mable Ringling Museum of Art opens to the public under the first executive director, A. Everett Austin, Jr.

1957 The Historic Asolo Theater, purchased in the late 1940s, is permanently installed in its own building adjacent to the north wing of the Museum of Art.

1996 Restoration begins on the Ringling winter residence, *Cà d'Zan*.

2000 Florida State University, under the leadership of President Sandy D'Alemberte, assumes governance of the Ringling Museum complex.

Cà d'Zan as Miss Havisham's decrepit ruin.

THE TRANSFORMATION BEGINS

Fortune changed for the Ringling Museum on July 1, 2000, when FSU assumed governance of the Museum, transferred to FSU from Florida's Department of State. The transition came as the brainchild of local Museum supporters – Bob Blalock of Bradenton and Bob Johnson of Sarasota prominent among them – who understood that Florida's University System offered benefits that could possibly save the failing institution. Among them, State Universities enjoyed two matching gift programs that could double contributions for new buildings and match money raised for endowment. Major universities also boasted large, efficient operating systems to assist with human resources, accounting, facility upkeep, and legal needs.

Meanwhile, under the leadership of President Talbot "Sandy" D'Alemberte, Florida State University had enjoyed its own cultural renaissance. Departments of Art Education, Drama, Dance, Film, and Music merited national rankings. But not many national critics visited FSU's main campus in Tallahassee, leaving academic excellence a "well kept secret." Since the early 1960s, FSU had established a presence in Sarasota by offering actor training and in 1973 establishing a master's degree in acting through a partnership with the independent Asolo Theater Company. For President D'Alemberte, the Ringling offered one of the most elegant settings for a college art museum in the world, with a collection worthy of comparison with those of Harvard and Yale.

But a major obstacle impeded the merger: the poor condition of the Museum itself. How could the university possibly devote its academic resources to alleviate the Museum's past neglect? Responsibility fell to the Florida Legislature to make the arrangement work, and so after long negotiations, promises were made that the State would provide funding to restore the Ringling Estate and the University pledged its expertise to develop a program of academic excellence at its new "cultural campus." Within months of the merger, President D'Alemberte, with FSU Provost Larry Abele, secured nearly $7 million to repair existing buildings, enhance infrastructure throughout the Ringling grounds, and complete the massive restoration of *Cà d'Zan*.

Rebirth of the Cà d'Zán Mansion

When the mansion's restoration was first planned in the mid-1990s, Ringling officials estimated the cost at $6 million – and were not even close. Much of the mansion's exterior assaulted by decades of wind and salt water required reconstruction. The rich marble terrace had to be rebuilt. Balusters and railings along the waterfront and in the majestic tower were restored, as were many of the decorative terracotta ornaments that paid tribute to the palaces of Venice. Windows were replaced and openings sealed. A new terracotta tile roof was installed. And by 1999, the exterior had been saved.

The second phase of restoration made good the Museum's commitment that the damage sustained through Cà d'Zan's neglect would never recur. The Museum installed a new air-handling system to assure constant temperature and humidity. A new security system was added, as were fire-suppression systems. Old wiring and plumbing were also replaced. Together, these improvements provided the level of environmental and safety control to meet modern museum standards.

FSU and the new management team led the final phase of restoration. Since the time of Mable Ringling, the interiors had undergone dramatic change, as furniture was replaced, walls painted

in new colors, and whole rooms transformed in manners that, 70 years later, would hardly have been recognized by Mrs. Ringling herself. Archival photographs were used to assess the original look of each room, and paint samples taken to determine precise colors. Original paintings and furnishings were retrieved from storage and restored, re-gilded, or provided with new fabric as necessary. Hungarian born illustrator and Ziegfeld Follies set designer, Willy Pogany's ceiling murals and other large-scale paintings were restored by international teams of conservators. Craftsmen cleaned and repainted original moldings and other ornaments, while volunteers expertly fabricated new lace for the necessary trims. Carpets and area rugs were conserved or replaced; the chandelier Ringling acquired from the Waldorf Astoria was cleaned and repaired; even clothing preserved from the Ringlings' wardrobe was moved back into the closets and drawers.

In the end, some $15 million – more than double the initial estimate – was spent to return *Cà d'Zan* back to the spirit of the Roaring Twenties. The mansion was reopened in April of 2002, raising attendance nearly fifty percent in the first year, and reestablishing *Cà d'Zan* as one of America's architectural treasures. It would also, in hindsight, serve as testimony to the prohibitive cost of deferring needed maintenance.

Repairs for the Museum of Art and Landscaping for the Estate

Elsewhere on the Ringling Estate, State funding appropriated in 2002 addressed badly needed items of deferred maintenance. A new roof for the Museum solved the leakage that had threatened irreplaceable paintings and the historic structure. The marble surface of the Loggia was restored to eliminate the water seepage that had caused years of decay. Access was improved with the installation of a lift from the original Art Museum building to the temporary exhibition galleries. The installation of a new, campus-wide security system protected holdings to the fullest extent possible.

Waters had not flown through two fountains in the Museum Courtyard for years. *The Fountain of Tortoises*, one of three replicas of the Piazza Mattei in Rome, and the *Oceanus Fountain*, copied from the 16th century original by Giovanni Bologna in Florence's Boboli Gardens, required restoration estimated in the $100s of thousands. With bids far too high, an ingenious idea to use a plumbing device that scoped the piping as angioplasty in hospitals cleans human veins was developed. It was done so affordably that the project won a state-wide "Davis Productivity Award" for saving money for the State of Florida.

Finally, Museum staff worked to restore the once-beautiful landscaped grounds. Horticulturist Ron Mallory made Mable Ringling's Rose Garden a personal pursuit, reviving the beds with new irrigation systems and recruiting volunteers to tend a spectacular garden that would earn accreditation from the All-America Rose Selections in 2004. The Museum also developed its own test garden for national rose certification. Elsewhere, members of Sarasota's Founders Circle – a garden club that once boasted Mable Ringling among its first president and members – contributed funds to restore the grounds surrounding *Cà d'Zan* to their original elegance, planting Royal Palms to line the regal walkway leading to the mansion. In partnership with Sarasota's Driftwood Circle Garden Club, volunteers and staff restored Mable Ringling's Secret Garden, turning the once-overgrown plot into an oasis of greenery and color.

EXPANSION FOR THE 21ST CENTURY

The neglect that had caused the original Ringling structures to deteriorate came with another challenge. Over the decades that major museums throughout North America had expanded, the Ringling buildings remained stagnant. Aside from the west wing of the Museum of Art, built in 1966 to house traveling exhibitions, the Museum library and provide office space for a small staff, the Museum had hardly grown at all.

Visitors were required to purchase tickets in the old Art Museum lobby, but the small space forced lines out the door and on busy days, outside the Museum grounds. With over two thirds of the Museum's visitors being tourists, there was no room for an orientation gallery, nor a place to welcome school groups. The Huntington Gallery at the entrance to the Museum served for a short while as a store, while a small restaurant built in the 1970s lacked space to serve all visitors. The Art Library of more than 65,000 volumes occupied an over-crowded space built for half that amount. Art storage was at capacity and located in a room barely over sea level – exposing valuable collections to the ravages of Florida's hurricane season. Staff was spread around the estate, some housed in trailers and others lodged in rented offices 2.5 miles away. There were no classrooms and only a small meeting space, requiring galleries to be closed to accommodate large groups. In short, the Museum had outgrown itself decades over, and desperately needed new facilities to fulfill its aspirations.

Circus Museum

Tibbals Learning Center

Guest Cottage

Asolo
Theater

Asolo Center
For the
Performance Arts

Reception
Pavilion

Ca' d'Zan
Gate

Ca' d'Zan

Bus
Parking

Renovated Ringling Landscape

Expa...
M...
Pa...

New Exhibition Galleries

Ringling
Museum of Art

Renovated West Wing

Restored Entry Boulevard

Center for Art History Research

FSU / Ringling Center for the Cultural Arts
master site plan

Evolution of the Master Plan

Even in the mid 1990s, as restoration of *Cà d'Zan* began, the Museum's board recognized the need for new facilities. Architect E. Verner Johnson and Associates of Boston was retained to finalize a master plan that had started in the 1980s to respond to the urgent need for collection storage space, more staff offices, educational facilities, and visitor amenities. The Johnson plan projected the programming needs of the Museum and outlined the footprints of the required buildings. Central to the plan was the concept of growing at the edges of the property, so that new structures would not compete with the natural beauty of the original Ringling Estate. The plan also envisioned an educational complex on a site to the south that was part of neighboring New College of Florida, but owed to the Ringling as part of a prior land exchange that had allowed the College's library to be built on an outcrop of Ringling land north of the Estate. Some ideas, such as a building new storage space at the prominent frontage along Bay Shore Road, appeared impractical. Nevertheless, the Johnson proposal served to illustrate the Museum's desperate need for space, and provided a structure for the plan that Florida State University would eventually refine and fulfill.

Soon after assuming governance, Florida State University engaged a firm from Orlando to assess the Johnson plan and suggest improvements. FSU also conducted its own needs assessment and in 2002 hired HOK and its lead architect from the Tampa office, Yann Weymouth, to "verify" the master plan.

The selection of HOK was somewhat unusual then for a major museum, given the trend among museums to hire "signature architects" (Frank Gehry, Santiago Calatrava, Daniel Libeskind, and others) whose celebrity and distinct architectural idioms were establishing new buildings as among the most valuable work of art in the collection. HOK was better known for sports stadiums, arenas, and corporate offices that mirrored its community and surroundings. But Weymouth, being new to the firm, came with over 20 years of experience with I. M. Pei, having assisted with designs for the National Gallery's East Wing, renovation of the Louvre in Paris, and plans to expand the Metropolitan Museum of Art in New York. His experience offered an understanding of museum procedures and aesthetic needs that would eventually provide exceptionally serviceable floor plans and beautiful galleries for the display of art.

While recognizing the basic principles of the master plan, Weymouth made some important changes. First, he abandoned proposals to graft a new visitors entrance to the front of the Museum of Art, envisioning instead a separate Visitors Pavilion on the northeast end of the Estate, directly behind the historic *Cà d'Zan* Gate. He moved art storage south to the education center on New College property.

And as his most brilliant proposal, he used Ringling's architect John Phillip's original plans as the basis for his exterior design of the new art galleries, in effect fulfilling John Ringling's own aspirations for the Museum. In a subtle and ingenious way, Weymouth became for the Ringling Museum the anti-signature architect, adopting for his architectural vernacular the vocabulary of the original Ringling Estate, and subordinating his exteriors to the original Ringling structures.

Landscape architect David Sachs of EDAW, Inc. of Miami, worked with HOK to develop a long-range plan for the grounds that emphasized historic preservation of the existing site while bringing out the inherent beauty of the 66-acre bayfront estate.

The Tibbals Learning Center

The vision for a new circus museum came from a partnership between collector and circus historian Howard Tibbals, creator of the world's largest scale model of the Ringling circus, and President D'Alemberte, who realized the importance of circus entertainment in the academic study of American culture. The two agreed to design a 30,000 square foot, stand-alone building to house the 3,800-square-foot *Howard Bros. Model Circus*, circus posters, and exhibitions on circus history. Financial arrangements leveraged the matching potential of university funding sources. Mr. Tibbals and local contributors raised the $6.5 million necessary to fund design and construction, but the monies themselves were split: half were earmarked for the building and matched through Florida's Alec P. Courtelis Capital Facilities Matching Trust Fund for State University buildings; remaining funds were designated for endowment, and later matched by the State's program for endowment gifts. Because of its relationship with FSU, the Museum was able to parlay construction funds into a new building and a separate endowment designated toward maintenance of the facility and model, programming, exhibits, and the curatorial support necessary to operate a first-rate circus museum.

Harvard, Jolly, Clees, Toppe Architects, of St. Petersburg, were retained to design the building, partner John Toppe taking the lead. His plan called for an oblong shaped building to wrap around the *Howard Bros. Model Circus*, with galleries on both floors for exhibits. Howard Tibbals' gift agreement called for features especially evocative of the original circus show, such as a tented entrance, colorful flags surrounding the building, and an entablature inscribed with the names of the most prominent circus show owners – Forepaugh, Bailey, Ringling, and Feld, among others. As master planner, Yann Weymouth collaborated with the architect, recommending walls made of pink-sand from Canada that would unite the new building with established Ringling architecture.

He also set the elevator and stairs in a separate cylinder, intending that it would conveniently serve a second, phase two building when the time for additional expansion came.

The Tibbals Learning Center, as it came to be called, doubled the size of the existing Circus Museum, offering interactive exhibits for children and families, as well as rare materials for scholars and historians. The centerpiece is the exquisitely crafted model circus, the largest of its kind in the world. Accurate to the tiniest of details, the *Howard Bros. Circus* consists of more than 44,000 separate pieces including 1,300 performers, musicians, and workers; more than 800 animals; 7,000 folding chairs; and 900 sets of silverware on tables in the dining tent. A scale model of Knoxville's railroad yard sets the scene in Mr. Tibbals' native Tennessee, the railway filled with empty flatbed cars recently unloaded. Across the span of an open field spread the circus tents themselves – a miniature tent city with dinning and cooking tents, a laundry tent and area for blacksmiths, dressing areas, practice rings, the menagerie, side show, and the big top itself. Animated features, programmed sound, and vintage video footage bring life to the display, as does a timed light sequence that shows off the model at night, lighted from within.

On the ground floor, a poster gallery presents circus graphics in specially designed cases that use magnets to hang each work, saving the time and expense of matting and framing each piece. An entry foyer welcomes visitors, with an adjacent video gallery to introduce circus themes. Upstairs, a comprehensive display designed by Jack Rouse Associates traces the history of the circus from its roots in ancient Rome, through the European traveling shows, to British riding shows, through the era of the Ringing Bros. and Barnum & Bailey and the Wild West Shows, all the way to present day wonders such as the Big Apple Circus, Cirque du Soleil, and the Greatest Show on Earth, Ringling Bros. and Barnum & Bailey Circus.

The John M. McKay Visitors Pavilion
and Historic Asolo Theater

Respect for the original Ringling Estate led to Yann Weymouth's most original modification of the master plan: locating the Visitors Pavilion directly behind the original *Cà d'Zan* Gate House. In years past, cars zipped at dangerous speeds through the gate and up the road leading to *Cà d'Zan* and the former Banyan Café restaurant. The structure itself was failing, pieces of the roof having fallen to the ground below. HOK's solution was to restore the Gate House and transform it into the main pedestrian entrance to the Ringling Estate. The roadway's footprint was maintained, leading directly through the new structure. The grounds behind the Gate House were densely planted with tall pines and thick groves of bamboo, effectively hiding the new building behind nature – a radical departure from the attention-grabbing shapes of contemporary signature buildings.

After passing through the restored *Cà d'Zán* Gate House (converted into a security post), Museum guests enter the grand lobby of the Visitors Pavilion. With a vast bank of admission stations for faster service, the lobby also provides entry to the 2,800-square-foot Museum Store, the popular Museum restaurant *Treviso*, an orientation video theater, a children's gathering area and the restored Historic Asolo Theater.

The Visitors Center provides amenities never before available to Museum guests. A large variety of souvenirs, gifts, books and prints are available in the two-level Museum Store. Its focal point is a series of hanging translucent panels that display the main elements of the Ringling Estate. The second floor mezzanine, with its reading room for books on art and topics related to the Ringling's history, features a circus theme with rings on the ceiling that lead the eye through the glass wall otherwise separating the store from the lobby.

Treviso features outdoor seating overlooking two ponds and the entrance tent of the Circus Museum's Tibbals Learning Center. Indoor seating includes an area for private parties at the top of a stunning spiral staircase. Named in tribute to the Italian province that includes Sarasota's sister city Asolo, *Treviso* has quickly become a popular oasis for Ringling visitors and a destination where the general public can meet over a light snack or full meal.

The most stunning feature of the Visitors Pavilion is the restored Asolo Theater, the birthplace of Sarasota's vibrant performing arts community. Created in Asolo, Italy in 1798, the jewel-like theater was the trophy of the Museum's first director, A. Everett Austin, Jr., who hailed it as the very

A Museum Once Forgotten

heart of his museum: "It has come across the sea to become one of the most important exhibits in a museum noted for its dramatic and spectacular collection of Baroque paintings, and to serve as a brilliant setting for plays, concerts, lectures, and motion picture programs that are part of the cultural advantages the Ringling Museum offers to students of the fine arts, and to the public."

Funds to restore the Manley Building that once housed the theater had come to the Museum as part of the restoration plan. The newly appointed executive director, Dr. John Wetenhall, and President D'Alemberte of FSU together recognized that its location, in the center of the estate far from parking and other amenities, had serious flaws. They proposed relocation in the new Visitors Pavilion, where museum ticketing by day could become a box office at night, and where the adjacent restaurant and store could serve not only guests to the original Asolo, but theatergoers attending shows at the FSU Center for the Performing Arts, across the street. It was a gesture intended to transform the Museum into a cultural center, vibrant and active both day and night.

With restoration funds diverted to the Visitors Pavilion, the original panels were carefully removed and the Manley Building razed. A collaborative team of professionals, including Ringling Museum conservators, architects, curators, and construction experts, worked together to restore with meticulous precision every theater panel. The team removed dirt and grime, restored painted images, filled cracks between wooden panels, and replaced worn-away gilding to revive once again the theater's Rococo elegance.

Designed to honor a queen, the newly equipped theater is ideally suited for today's discerning patrons of the performing arts. Whether seated in the orchestra, or in the rising tiers of boxes, each audience member is afforded uncommon intimacy with the performers. As the houselights dim and the curtains part, the gilded ornamentation and simulated jewels gracing both proscenium and parapets reflect the brilliance of the artistry on stage.

In 2006, the Florida Legislature named the Visitors Pavilion in honor of the person most responsible for funding the Ringling Renaissance, former State Senator John M. McKay, to stand as lasting testimony to his vision and accomplishment.

A Museum Once Forgotten

The Education/Conservation Building

The administrative heart of the Master Plan is the 68,000-square-foot Education/Conservation Building, providing space to fulfill the expanded education mission of the Museum. It also houses the Museum's professional staff, formerly dispersed among a variety of buildings, rented spaces and temporary trailers, both on the estate and off-site. An open space office system was adopted by HOK to optimize square footage while at the same time providing numerous meeting rooms, small conference rooms, workspaces, and a computer training room for staff. The facility also features academic spaces for adult courses and graduate seminars, as well as meeting rooms for teacher-training and professional certification. Each classroom is equipped for distance learning, making the educational reach boundless.

Beyond unifying the professional staff, the building redresses a variety of concerns: inadequate space for the art library, a small conservation laboratory, and most urgent of all, art storage vaults and archives formerly located below the flood plane. The new Ringling Art Library, one of the largest in the southeast, provides a spacious reading room large enough to serve staff, Museum members, students, scholars, and visitors. There is ample space to house the 65,000 books, periodicals, and exhibition and auction catalogues previously housed in a room designed for half the amount. The second floor houses the Ringling Archives, preserving institutional documents as well as Ringling and circus history for the benefit of students and scholars from around the world.

Collection care now benefits from a state-of-the-art conservation laboratory, more than double the size of the old lab. Given sufficient space, the laboratory will have the capacity to serve regional institutions in addition to the Ringling's collection. Secure and climate-controlled storage facilities, located well above the "100-year" flood level, are equipped to preserve priceless art even if confronted with the ravages of Florida's hurricane season.

The Ulla R. and Arthur F. Searing Wing

Yann Weymouth's most deferential gesture to the vision of John Ringling came in the design of the new art galleries with its exterior based on the 1920s renderings by Ringling's architect, John Phillips. The original plans envisioned a wing extending from the northern Loggia of the Museum to house a Ringling School of Art (later founded independently in Sarasota and now thriving as one of America's leading schools of design). The building would be square, centered on a courtyard for sculpture. On the outside, an arcade would extend the Loggia of the original Museum, with a balustrade above like the original structure of the Museum of Art in all but the absence of monumental sculptures. The Weymouth plan modified Phillips' floorplan only in its location, the arcade extending the original loggia on axis, rather than set back as in the old drawing. The only other difference is at the eastern end, where HOK located a loading dock so that traveling exhibitions could be off-loaded mere meters from the galleries in which they will be displayed.

The interiors are thoroughly contemporary, presenting finished galleries suitable for the most demanding standards of 21st-century exhibition design. The building provides an additional 20,000 square feet of space for exhibitions, enabling many more objects from the Ringling's vast collection to be placed on public view. Spaces are equipped with ultra-sensitive climate controls, a comprehensive security system, flexible lighting for a variety of art forms, moveable walls, elegant bamboo and white oak flooring. There is even a basement directly below the loading dock for temporary storage of crates and supplies.

The Courtyard was designed to host social functions, such as exhibition openings and corporate parties. A well-equipped catering kitchen abuts the loading dock, with segregated air handling systems separate from those for art. A corridor provides access from the kitchen to the open space without passing through art galleries. The exterior of the Courtyard was left simple, in anticipation of a site-specific art installation to be installed at a later date.

Beyond new buildings, funds were invested in estate-wide projects aimed toward future efficiencies. A chilled water loop system was installed underground to connect all buildings through a central system, designed to reduce energy and equipment costs for decades to come. Neighboring New College of Florida partnered with the Museum by allowing the chiller units to be housed in the New College complex, in exchange for connecting New College's Caples Campus to the Ringling system. This cooperation decreased construction costs considerably, saved valuable space, and provided back-up chilled water for the College. In addition, three new retention ponds were landscaped with tropical vegetation. New pathways were laid for the convenience of pedestrians and riders of the Museum's courtesy trams. The Dwarf Garden, a beloved fixture of the Asolo Theater, was relocated beneath the imposing shade of a magnificent Banyan tree, to the south of the new Visitors Pavilion. Two rows of Royal Palms were planted along the Esplanade, providing a stately prominence for the entry to the Estate. John Ringling's statues of antique masterworks from the Chiurazzi foundry in Naples have been conserved and moved to the Courtyard and Loggia of the Museum of Art. Inside, art galleries have been reinstalled and an audio tour developed for the enjoyment of visitors. Wherever possible, the Museum's landscaping staff oversaw new plantings, even around construction sites, to save cost and assure lasting quality. Altogether, the Ringling Estate has been transformed.

The four new buildings of the master plan have doubled the size of the Ringling Museum, ranking it among the 20 largest art museums in North America. Over $56 million was invested in new structures, contributing more than 165,000 square feet of usable space. Added to the $21 million required to restore the Ringling's historic structures, the total investment in facilities and infrastructure exceeds $76 million. And there would be more.

Timeline

2002 *Cà d'Zan* restoration completed

2002 Restoration and expansion planning phase completed and *Ringling Now* campaign commences

2003 $42.9 million appropriated to the Museum and *Ringling Now & Forever* Campaign commences

2006 Opening of the John M. McKay Visitors Pavilion, Tibbals Learning Center and Education/Conservation building

2007 Opening of the Ulla R. and Arthur F. Searing Wing

EXPANDING THE VISION

Over time, the wisdom and accomplishment of the Ringling's master plan will be measured not by cost and square footage, but by the quality of exhibitions and cultural programs that the Museum provides. New educational spaces are slated to host an adult institute for cultural studies, making the Museum a destination point for cultural tourism and in-depth learning. Plans for a children's cultural camp during summers are also developing, in collaboration with FSU's nationally ranked Department of Art Education. Graduate semesters for museum studies have already begun, utilizing the museum as a laboratory for institutional "best practices" and as a springboard for students to begin museum careers. Programming in the Asolo Theater has expanded the Museum's cultural reach, generating collaborations among Sarasota's exceptionally strong performing arts community, and bringing theater, music, film and dance to the Ringling grounds. And of course, the mission-driven activities that most major museums pursue – mounting important exhibitions, refining collections, publishing, engaging visitors with collections, educating school children, and reaching out to underserved populations – continues with new energy, inspired by a rejuvenated environment.

The momentum of the Museum's recent success has also accelerated plans for new buildings. Recent gifts have made two important initiatives for art possible, and preparations for the next phase of the Circus Museum are underway.

A Rubens Gallery for the 21st Century: James Turrell's Skypiece

An open space exposed to the hot Florida sun, the Courtyard of the new Searing Wing was always envisioned as a space that should one day be enclosed. In 2004, the Museum's executive director, Dr. John Wetenhall, and architect Yann Weymouth met with artist James Turrell to explore the possibility of transforming the site into one of the artist's famed Skypieces. Inspired by the Ringling's history and the vast expanses posed by the enclosure, Turrell proposed doubling the height of the surrounding walls, from 22 to 44 feet, the upper half to form a box of pristine white, open in the center to the sky. Along the lower walls, foliage would be grown to create a tropical garden to surround viewers with native vegetation. Tilted benches would lead viewers gaze upward, toward an open square at the center of the space. During evening hours, the opening would evolve through a series of colors, from a pale, translucent blue through the richest of deep, dark blues, finally becoming a solid square of opaque black at night. At times of inclement weather or excessive heat, a retractable roof would cover the space and a show of subtly changing colored light would energize the area above with a radiant glow. And unlike other, smaller Skypieces by Turrell, this would be fully functional as a social space: a café by day and a venue for parties, educational functions, or museum openings by night. It would be a tour-de-force of contemporary art on an epic scale – over 5,000 square feet – designed to be every bit as inspiring as Ringling's original designs for his Rubens Gallery – a Rubens Gallery for our own time.

The Courtyard was engineered so that the expanded roof could be constructed at a later time, with air conditioning ducts incorporated in advance. Soon after completion in 2006, funds were received that have brought the proposal within reach.

Dr. Helga Wall-Apelt Gallery of Asian Art

In 2006, philanthropist and collector of Asian art Dr. Helga Wall-Apelt selected the Ringling Museum as the site to fulfill her vision of a center for Asian art. Founder of Sarasota's Museum of Asian Art, a facility formerly housed in rented space, Dr. Wall-Apelt had been seeking a permanent home for her collection and a venue for educational programming and scholarly pursuits to open the continent of Asia to the regional community. The Ringling Museum had already received in 2002 the renowned collection of Chinese ceramics assembled by Ira and Nancy Koger, making the Ringling a potentially ideal partner, especially given the State of Florida's matching gifts program. Inspired by the precedent of Howard Tibbals's gift, Dr. Wall-Apelt pledged to the Museum an $8 million contribution equal to the construction cost of a new building, half to be matched by the State for design and construction, the other to be matched for endowment to fund exhibitions and programs. In addition, the promised gift of her collection and future contributions have valued the gift in the range of $50 million.

A comprehensive renovation of the Museum's existing West Galleries (constructed in 1966) will form the core of the new space, with an entry pavilion to be added to the westernmost end. The Galleries will feature elegantly refurbished spaces for the display of the Koger ceramics and Dr. Wall-Apelt's extensive holdings that include a large and exquisite collection of Chinese jades, bronze Southeast Asian sculptures of the 18th and 19th centuries, and Cambodian stone figures dating to the 12th and 13th centuries. Representing nearly half a century of collecting, the collection has recently grown to include contemporary Asian art, and will continue to evolve in the years ahead.

Beyond the 10,000 square feet of gallery space, the 37,000-square-foot facility will include a study center for works on paper, meeting areas, art support space, and a classroom for children on the basement level. Across the pond from the new pavilion (as yet to be designed), plans call for the creation of an Asian tea garden. The Dr. Wall-Apelt Endowment for Asian Art will support curatorial staff, lectures, seminars, scholarly research, visits by guest scholars, internships, publications, exhibitions, acquisitions, public programs and other activities related to Asian art and culture.

More Circus Dreams

Recognizing that the original Circus Museum was old and beyond repair, the Tibbals Learning Center was built separately, some 50 yards to the east, with a vision of expansion later. The concept anticipated building a Phase II that would link the two buildings, and a final Phase III that would eventually replace the aged 1948 structure. Preliminary renderings by HOK's Yann Weymouth anticipate a continuation of the Tibbals building westward, with a large, spacious gallery to extend exhibition space and possibly a circus study center occupying the space above. Curatorial plans have already been drafted to dedicate the next phase of display to the history of circus acts, complimenting the history of circus owners in the Tibbals Learning Center. Acts will be linked to principles of science, for the benefit of children who visit, just as the history of circus was linked to a timeline of American history. The concept is to elevate circus display to a portal of learning in a variety of fields.

When the time comes for the original Circus Museum to be replaced, the new facility will enlarge again the space for circus display, and include a performance ring for live circus demonstrations and films about the American Circus. Exhibition plans envision displays dedicated to the backlot, the circus side-show, and other behind-the-scenes activities.

A unique feature that will add another dimension to the Circus Museum is the restoration of John Ringling's personal railcar, the Wisconsin, in which he traveled the United States from 1905, shortly after marrying Mable, until the Ringlings purchased the Jomar, another rail car. Its relocation in the new building will assure that Ringling history remains the centerpiece of Circus display.

Beyond major construction projects, plans call for a variety of improvements to the Ringling grounds, as well as improved visitor amenities such as added parking. In the years ahead, landscaping will help to beautify and develop the Estate's scenic waterfront, highlighting panoramic views toward Longboat Key and the lavish Florida sunsets. There are even plans for an outdoor performance stage, and possibly a wedding pavilion, but those are likely to remain visions for a more distant future.

ENDOWMENT: FINANCIAL FOUNDATIONS FOR FUTURE SUCCESS

The most remarkable aspect of the Ringling's building boom is that it nearly did not happen. Thanks to the leadership of Senate President John M. McKay, Senator Lisa Carlton, and the local delegation, the State Budget for 2002-2003 included $42.9 million in the Florida State University allocation to fund the entire Ringling/FSU Master Plan. Within weeks of passage, however, the funding appeared in jeopardy. By allocating construction funds in the University's base budget, the Legislature had shielded them from a governor's veto; however, the tactic meant that they could legally be spent on any university building project. It soon became apparent that political pressure was forming to divert the money to the Tallahassee campus. So as the Ringling Board entered its fiscal year with new officers, a darkly looming political challenge appeared: find a way to secure the allocated funds, or lose them and tarnish the entire FSU relationship, likely delaying the Master Plan for years to come.

The "Ringling Now" $42.9 Million Challenge

The newly appointed chairman of the Ringling Board of Directors, Vern Buchanan, personally dedicated much of the summer to broker a solution, traveling to Tallahassee to meet with political leaders and university officials. The basis for an agreement rested in the funding model for the Tibbals Learning Center: new buildings should be accompanied by endowment sufficient to support the curatorial and educational programs that would take place within.

Encouraging cooperation between FSU President Sandy D'Alemberte, Chairman of the FSU Board of Trustees John Thrasher, and Governor Jeb Bush, Chairman Buchanan forged an agreement in the form of a challenge: half of the appropriation would come to the Museum up front, while the other half held in reserve, payable with a two-part commitment from the Ringling Board that 1) would raise $50 million for endowment within the next five years, and that 2) the first $10 million must be raised during the first year. Failure to meet the goal would lead to forfeiture of the remaining construction funds. The one-year time limit commenced immediately, upon approval by the FSU Board of Trustees on September 20, 2002, providing no period for planning a campaign. Perhaps more daunting, over sixty years of operation had left the Museum with less then $5 million in total endowment funds. How would $10 million be raised in a single year?

The "Ringling Now Challenge," as it came to be called, engaged the entire community, as civic leaders and philanthropists realized the extraordinary opportunity within reach. Beyond the prospect of nearly $21 million in construction funds, major gifts to endowment also qualified for State matching funds, providing compelling leverage for major gifts. People also came to realize the Museum's economic potential to support regional tourism, as well as its educational and cultural value to the entire community. It was a one-time challenge that community leaders determined was simply too attractive to miss.

A lead gift of $1 million by Bob and Diane Roskamp, followed by another $1 million pledge by Vern and Sandy Buchanan, inspired $1 million-plus commitments by the Selby Foundation, and the Amicus Foundation. Assisted by the FSU Foundation's fundraising professionals, the local Board of Directors hosted numerous lunches, dinners and cocktail parties to introduce potential contributors to the plan, and in so doing, excited the community about the Ringling's promising future. The campaign also benefited from 100% board member participation, contributions by the entire Members' Council and over 350 other gifts. By August, the $10 million goal had been reached. Additional gifts, including a $2 million commitment from Mr. and Mrs. John F. Cuneo, Jr. and an in-kind gift by Mark P. Famiglio, brought the total to nearly $13 million by the final deadline. At its September 19, 2003 meeting, the Florida State University Board of Trustees voted to release the balance of the $42.9 million appropriation; the FSU partnership with Ringling was secured; and the Ringling's Renaissance became a reality.

In the years that followed, amidst the massive construction project, Museum leaders continued raising endowment. Major gifts came from Mr. and Mrs. Marvin I. Danto. Philanthropist Ulla R. Searing pledged $6.5 million (1/2 the construction cost) to name the new Art Galleries. And in January of 2006, the pledge by Dr. Helga Wall-Apelt brought the campaign over the $50 million goal. By the time construction of the new buildings was completed in the Autumn of 2006, the Museum Board of Directors had made good on its word, having raised a total over $56 million toward its endowment pledge.

Even with such extraordinary recent success, funding challenges remain. To achieve real long-term stability, salary lines for curators, educators, and top administrators still must be endowed, as should programming needs for children and adults. Exhibitions require underwriting and acquisition funds must be established to help the art and circus collections grow. But even while acknowledging future needs, the financial prospects of the Museum have never looked better.

HONOR ROLL: FOR THOSE WHO MADE THE TRANSFORMATION POSSIBLE

The lists that follow recognize the many generous contributors who have helped to fund new buildings for the Museum and the endowments necessary to support them. In addition to the honor roll of financial donors, we have added three more. First, the Ringling Board of Directors has worked tirelessly, and with its members' reputations on the line, to fulfill the $50 million endowment challenge and see to the timely completion of all new buildings. Board chairs Senator Marlow W. Cook, Carolyn G. Johnson, Vernon G. Buchanan, Dorothy C. Jenkins, and Alice W. Rau deserve special mention for their leadership during the FSU transition. Secondly, the leadership of Florida State University – President T.K. Wetherell, Provost Larry Abele, Chief Financial Officer John Carnaghi, Vice President Lee Hinkle, and President Emeritus Talbot "Sandy" D'Alemberte – must be acknowledged for their unwavering support and encouragement, without which we could not possibly have prospered. And finally, the Museum's professional staff must all be recognized as individual contributors, having forgone the higher wages of the private sector to dedicate their working lives to the betterment of the Ringling Museum, and the many, many people it serves.

$1,000,000 AND UP

Amicus Foundation
Anonymous #242
Mary Tilley Bessemer*
Vern and Sandra Buchanan and
  Sarasota Ford
John and Herta Cuneo, Jr.
Marvin and Betty Danto
Mark and Jennie Famiglio
Robert and Diane Roskamp
Ulla R. Searing
William G. Selby and Marie Selby
  Foundation
The State of Florida
Howard and Janice Tibbals
Dr. Helga Wall-Apelt

$500,000 - $999,999

Keating Family Foundation
Winona Lowe*
Peter and Pamela Vogt

$100,000 - $499,999

Armour Family Foundation
Barbara and Martin Arch
Dr. and Mrs. Gene Armstrong
A. Alexandra Jupin and John Bean
Trevor Bell
Robert and Marlene Blalock
Frank Brunckhorst III
Linnie E. Dalbeck
  Memorial Foundation
Betty Brooks Doss
Frank E. Duckwall Foundation
Mr. and Mrs. David M. Essenfeld
Koni and Cary Findlay

Florida Department of State -
  Div. of Administrative Svcs.
Mr. and Mrs. Arnold L. Greenfield
Stanley Goldman
Gulf Coast Community Foundation
  of Venice
Lillian Huisking
The Huisking Foundation
Dorothy and Charles Jenkins, Jr.
Unni and Philip Kaltenbacher
Robert E. and Beverly L. Koski
Gunther Less
Gale and Tom MacCabe, Jr.
Estate of Joseph A. McGarrity
Joan and Ira Mendell
Kenneth and Myra Monfort
  Charitable Foundation
National Endowment for the Arts
Richard H. and Betty Watt Nimtz
Publix Super Markets Charities
Alice W. Rau
John and Tana Sandefur
Arnold and Barbara Siemer
Robert and Joyce Tate
Steve and Stevie Wilberding

$50,000 - $99,999

Anonymous #241
Susan Brainerd, Ph.D. and Alan Quinby
E. Rhodes and Leona B. Carpenter
  Foundation
Warren and Margot Coville
Rod and Kay Heller II
Janet and Don Hevey
Walter Serwatka and Connie Holcomb
Icard Merrill Cullis Timm Furen & Ginsburg
Phyllis and Chuck Savidge

DONORS
Donor List accurate as of Dec. 1, 2006

Judy and Les Smout
Lorin and Harriet Steiff
Tarr Charitable Family Foundation
John and Anna Maria Troiano
Jack Woodward, Jr.

$10,000 - $49,999

Stephen Leonard Johnston Adam Trust
Anonymous #243
Miranda and Robert Anderson
Myrna and David Band
Bank of America Client Foundation
Laura and G. Guyton Carkener
The Harriet and Raymond Brush
  Charitable Foundation
Margaret and Bob Christopher
Community Foundation of
  Greater Lakeland Inc.
Nancy and Marlow Cook
Mary Ann Stankiewicz and David Ebitz
Leon and Margaret Ellin
Louis and Gloria Flanzer
Founders Circle of Sarasota Garden Club
Jane and Robert Geniesse
Barbara and Julian Hansen
W. Paul Hoenle and Ursula Heitmann
Linda L. and David W. Houze
Barbara Jarabek
Christine Jennings

DONORS

Carolyn and Bob Johnson
Senator Bob and Pat Johnson
Lynden and Kristen Lyman
Dr. Richard and Francelle* Marcus
Esther Mertz
Eleanor Merrit-Darlington
Herbert G. McKay*
Michael Saunders & Company
Simon Portnoy
James and Sharon Roth
Marshall Rousseau
Marcia Rubin*
Donna and Mark Salzberg
Catherine and David Straz
Robert Stuffings
SunTrust Bank, Gulf Coast
Tom and Lavinia Touchton
Margaret and Leslie* Weller
Estate of Elsa James Zelley

$1,000 - $9,999

Henri and Harriet Arnold
Valliere Auzenne
Margie and Chuck Barancik
Elaine and James Barnett
Beers Skanska Inc.
Sharon and Greg Betterton
Anne and Walter Bladstrom
Susan and James Buck
Catherine Cabaniss

John Camp
Jerry and Gerry Clevenger
Uta and Arland Christ-Janer
Marjorie Coley
Colonial Bank
The Community Foundation
    for Greater Atlanta, Inc.
Community Foundation
    of Sarasota County, Inc.
The Robert & Marcia M. Costello
    Family Foundation, Inc.
Eileen Donovan
Chris and Walter Eisle, Jr.
Goldie Feldman
Richard and Suellen Field
Leila Gompertz
William and Ruth Gulick
Lois Harrison and Homer Hooks
Melvin Herrin
Jerome and Geraldine Hilmes
David and Muriel Hinkle
Allen and Nina Hughes
The Jelks Family Foundation
Irwin and Sharon Jones
Thomas Kaiser
Jay and Becky Kaiserman
Pauline Kahn
Janet and Stanley Kane
Alexander Kirkpatrick
Selma Klingenstein
Sandra and Stan Krawetz
Jenny Lassen
Mildred Lint
Claire Baker and Lee Lolkema
Debe and Jed Lykes III
Jane Marvin
Peter and Janice Mattina
John and Michelle McKay

Britton and Allen Miller
Jim and Lizabeth Moore II
Dick Mottino
The New York Times Company
    Foundation, Inc.
Richard Newdick
Helene and Eugene Noble
Paula Parrish and Donald C. Shulman*
Fred and Janet Pfenning III
Ellen Piers
Earl and Betty Pollock
Virginia W. Powel Trust
Nancy and Peter Reinheimer, Jr.
Didi and Sandy Rief III
Helen and Edward Rhawn
Harry and Sandra Robinson, Jr.
Linda and Robert Rosenbluth
Sandy and David Rossin
Joseph Russo, Jr.
Willard Saperston
Jennifer and Larry Saslaw
Mary and Buddy Savary
Pamela Sher
Janet and Ralph Sieve
Alice and Charles Schmutz
Philippe Roth and Jeremy Schwimmer
George Skestos
Lonabelle Spencer
Standford Nitzche Ltd.
Robert and Elaine Stein
Patricia and Charles Steward
Louise Sulzberger*
SouthTrust Bank
Anne and Adrian Swain
Kathleen Teso
Gerald Lippes and Jody Ulrich
Everett and Deborah Walk
Estate of David C. Weeks

Dr. John and Tanya Wetenhall
Roxie White
Albert and Jane Wohlers
The Woodward Foundation, Inc.

$500 - $999

Martha and Terence Allen
Bank of America Foundation
Margaret Bates
R.M. Bourque
Roz and Sam Brott
Tom and Katherine Cook
Anna Copeland
Harriet and Donald Duetsch
Gloria Duffy
The Eakins Press Foundation
Jack Goldsmith
Lucy Harrison
Carolyn Hirsch
Charlotte G. Howland
Betty Jane and Robert Keil
Marian and Richard Kessler
Tess Koncick and Donald Malawsky
Jane and Joel Larus
Betty and Alvin Lindenberg
Jane and Carlyle Luer
Jean Maguire
Ron Mallory
Manatee Community Foundation
Grant and Lisa Martin
Dorothy Morrison
Eugene Oberdorfer
Thomas and Marjorie Peter
Peggy and Donald Roberts
Susan and Malcolm Robinson
Evan and Janet Robinson
E. Scott Rosenbaum and Gretchen Piper

Dorothy Russell
Sarah Sanford-Miller
Catherine Scalera
Carolyn and Robert Schneebeck
Sandra and Charles Schneider
Showfolks Of Sarasota Tent No 122 CFA
Jane Smiley
Nancy and Donald Sontag
Stevenson Architects, Inc.
Arthur Wiedinger, Jr.

$100 - $499

Jean Adelson
Charles and Vicki Alkire
Alumnae Association of
   Kappa Kappa Gamma
Jesse Amass
Nancy Anderson
Anonymous #0249
Brian and Barbara Bain
Michael and Joanne Bander
Barbara Banks
Donald and Dorothy Bardo
Herbert and Jean Barth
James and Nancy Bass
Alex and Linda Beavers, Jr.
Corinne and John Beggy
Sybil Berkwitz
Harvey and Erika Bowermaster
Elvira Bowers
James and Joan Breen
E. Ann Brownell
Bonnie Bryant
Natalie Buchman
Wayne and Helen Bundrick
Harvey Burstein
Jean Burtis

DONORS

John Carroll
Alexander and Irene Cass
Robert and Dindy Chalphin
Dorothy Chandler
Virginia Chase
James and Gloria Clendon
C. Beatty and Helen Collins
Sandra Collins
Erika and Edward Corpron
Marilyn and Michael Counen
Cynthia and Allen Cudworth
Lynn De Groote
Peggy Day
Marie and Vincent De Lisi
Raymond and Ilda Deming
Ellen Dennis
Hans and Elfi Dierks
Ward and Louann Dillon
Marie Dimino
Donna Dolan
Edward Doolan
Douglas Dyment
Alfred Ginewsky and Mimi Edlin
James and Ellie Endriss
Bernice and Robert Eldredge
Sharon and Ronald Erickson
Ruth Erlandson
Fred and Josephine Falkner
Ernest and Ruth Feldman
Karen and Steven Feldman

DONORS

Fine Arts Society of Sarasota
John Fisher
Rod and Anne Fletcher
John Foster and Andrea Dimino
Allie Freedman
Elizabeth Funston
George Gall
W. Miles and Dana Gentry, Jr.
Goldman, Sachs & Co.
Sylvie Gould
Sally Graven
Donald and Karen Grierson
Roger and Lynne Grimshaw
Marc and Martha Grinberg
Carol-Jane and Joseph Guardino
Sergio Gutman
Lois Haber
Richard and Judith Haney
Melissa Hanna
Philip Hartley
Christine and Frank Heider
Lawrence and Mary Hepburn
Wayne Hepburn
Shirley Hess
Marjorie and Austin Hines
Ann Hollins
Marilyn and John Huebner
Jack and Betty Jo Hunkele
Roberta and Paul Ingrassia
Irongate Realty, Inc.
Carroll and Susan Johnson
Paul Johnson
The S. Irwin Kamin Foundation
R.D. Keith
James Kennady
Marilynn Kenyon
Mark Ketchum

Frances B. Knight
Fred and Sylvia Knight
Charles and Janet Koons
Roland and Karen Kopp
Ernest and Alisa Kretzmer
Floyd and Marjorie Kruger
Connie and Bill Kundrat, Jr.
Lorne and Mary Langlois
Betty-Ann and Louis Landman
Larry Geimer & Associates, CPAs, P.A.
Robert and Judith Lauer
Dixie Lee
Phyllis and James LeTellier
Mary Lou Loughlin
Donna Mann
Bluma Marcus
Michael Matchitto
John Markham III
John Mayer and Jeanne Hutchison
Walter and Donna Maytham
John and Nike McBride
Nike B. and James McKechnie, Jr.
Arden McKennee
Doug McVicar and Frumie Selchen
Lillian Meckler
John and Cathie Meyer
Millcreek Community Hospital
David and Anne Miller
Stanley Miller
Moore School
Marjorie Moote
Earl and Ann Mumford
Richard and Sally Myers
Gary Myron
Peggy and Philbin Nardone
Beatrice Newman
James and Harriette Norman

Steven and Harriet Osterweis
John Papadopulo
Robert and Jean Parker, Jr.
Caryn and Stephen Patterson
Donald and Dianne Patterson
Franklin and Patricia Peck
LeRoy and Gladys Peckham
Fred and Lee Pfenning, Jr.
Donald and Marjorie Piersol
Yvonne Pinkerton
Shirley Ramspeck
Judy and Warren Rider
Dale and Evelyn Riker
Norton and Jacqueline Rock
Marguerite Romzick
Mildred and Robert Rosenthal
Arlene Rothman
Ethel and Gregg Royer
Joyce and Harris Rubin
Carolyn Sanders
Donald and Patricia Savage
Patricia Schemm and Lynn Harding
C. Schmidt-Shilling
Judith Schrier
Roselyn Sedlezky
William and Kathleen Seider
Renee Sheade
Frederick Shibley, Jr.
Maureen and Stanley Siegel
Ellen Silkes

DONORS

Andy and Marcy Singleton
Janet and Bob Steele
Mildred and Paula Stein
Russell and Sharon Stephens
Marvin and Patricia Stucky
R. H. Suguitan
Henry Sutton
Barbara and Bob Swan
Timothy and Dawn Tibbals
Barbara Tilley
Vincent and Linda Vertefeuille
Barnes Walker, Chartered
Joyce Waterbury
Norton and Judith Waterman
Richard and Denise Watermeier
Elinor Welson
Whitehall Quality Homes, Inc.
Lucy Wind
Tracy Winkler
Roy and Sondra Witherington
Virginia Wright
James and Patricia Wu

$5 - $99

Georgette Abell
Libby Adelman
John and Gwen Albritton
Edna Alexander
Robert and Beth Anderson
Janet Andres

Leigh and Betty Andrews
Judy Axe
Elden Bailey
Robert and Janet Beitle
Edwin and Janet Bennett
Lois Bennett and Milt Felsen
Marge and Eben Blackett
Charles Blake
Stephen and Elizabeth Booth
Annie Bragg
Theodore Brasch and Jenn Hathaway
Andrew and Debbie Brooman
Aenita Burns
Marge Canfield
Mary Cantu
Patrica Caproon
Mollie Cardamone
James Carides
Lawrence Cash
Marguerite Chabau
Carol Chance
Katherine and Stanley Chichester
Allan and Julie Chytrowski
Pamela and John Clise
Jean Cochran and Richard Collier
Juanita Cochrane
Tufts and Richard Colwell
V.E. and Laura Copes
Diane and Claire Cory
Hazel Crofoot
John and Shirley Dane
Soli and Jo Anne Dastur
Herbert and Mary Ellen DeGroft
Zita and Milford Desenberg, Jr.
Shirley Dinkin
Fay Donaldson
Gerald and Charlotte Dratch
Irvin and Eileen Drury

John and Suzy Dryud
William and Verla Ebert
Margaret Ellison
Karen and Dennis Ellsworth
Kathy Espe
Red and Donna Falzone
Rick and Coni Fawley
W. F. and Gloria Feely
Grace Ford
Elizabeth Forlenza
G. C. Society For Humanistic Judaism
Robert Garbutt and Betty Casey
Bea Gartenberg
Jack and Jeanette Gay
Dan and Cheryl Gerren
Darwin and Kathryn Gervais
Luigi Giannattasio and Monica DiMattei
GM Sunseekers Club
Paul and Eva Goetz
Lynne Gold-Bikin
Henry and Katherine Goldman
Sommers Gostin
Murray and Ruth Grain
Louise Gregory and Ann Bement
Matthew and Autumn Gress
Mary Grummon
Francoise Hack
Sharon Hadary
Orlon and Emma Hall
Valerie Halla
Jeanne and Norman Harris
Ruth Hart-Schneider
Olivia and Robert Haynes
Thomas and Lucy Heller
Kenneth and Janice Hexdall
Adele and Sheldon Holland
John Hooten
Isabelle and Herbert Horowitz

A Museum Once Forgotten

DONORS

Esther and Irving Kammen
Robert and Patricia Karz
Steven Katz
Jo Ann Keene
David Kellogg
Virginia Keyes
Judy Kirchmeir
Philip and Marcia Kleinschmidt
Carol Kopeck
Nancy and Donald Kopf
Paul Kruezer
Ruth Kruglick
Bradley and Norma Kwenski
Iris and Bob La Joie
Elizabeth Lane
Lassus Wherley & Associates, P.C.
James and Susan Lanier
Alice and Louise Lavitt
Judy and Gerald Levinson
Gladys Lippincott
James and Judith Liston
Brian Livsey
Doris Lommel
Robert and Caryl Magnus
Nell Maha
Sandra and Neil Malamud
Louis and Ann Marie Marinaccio
Harriet Marks
Elizabeth Marx and Jean Wyre
Louise Mazius
Mary McFate
Marcia and Richard McLaughlin
Bill and Anne McSweeney
Wilda Meier
Sandra Melinkoff
W. Richard and Mary Mertz
Polly Meyer
Lois Mitchell

Model A. Restorers Club
Vincent Monti
Eadith Morales
Robert and Jo Ann Morrison
Beverly and Barbara Carol Mulconry
Marie and Sam Nemazie
Shirley and John Nilsen
A.J. and Barbara Noftz
Muriel O'Neil and Gertrude Hight
Marvin and Muriel Ostroff
Doris Palmer
Elin Parks
Michael and Julie Pender, Jr.
Robert and Donna Perkins
James and Victoria Philpitt
Esther Philpott
Irene Pospieski
Micheline Pulli
Mary Reading
Isabel and Milton Rauch
Frances Roach
Flori Roberts
Jean and Marvin Robertson
Edna Rosenbaum
Audrey Sagers and Jeffrey Steele
Barbara Sanderson
Joan Sapstein
Jane and Emily Sattler
Vincent and Patricia Scullin
Mary Seymour
Melvin and Jane Shepherd
Dianne and George Shipley
James and Linda Singletary
Frank and Mary Siriani
Eva Slane
Stanley Smitten
Nancy Sorenson and Jean Hessey
Doris Spangenberg

Robert Stanko
Charles Stephenson
Sunshine Region Antique Automobile
  Club of America
Francesca and James Sutherland
Barbara Sweeney
Desneiges Terrien
Ann and Robert Texido
Ellen and Joseph Timko
Mary Jane and Jack Tolpa
Charles and Geraldine Topp
Susan Tuchow
R.R. Tuleya, Jr.
Lillian Vanko
Daphne and Bill Walker, Jr.
Emily Wallis
Beatrice Warfield
Elizabeth and William Wildhack
Joan and Robert Wilson
Evelyne Winans
Sherry and Harold Wolfe
Sally and Robert Wyner
Dominic Yodice

*Deceased

STAFF

FLORIDA STATE UNIVERSITY LEADERSHIP

T.K. Wetherell, President
Talbot "Sandy" D'Alemberte,*
  President Emeritus
Larry Abele, Provost
John Carnaghi, Vice President
  Finance & Administration
Lee Hinkle, Vice President
  University Relations
Jim Smith, Chairman of
  FSU Board of Trustees
John Thrasher,* Former Chairman of
  FSU Board of Trustees
Jeff Robison*
Sally McRorie
Perry Crowell
Paul Strouts
Charles Rasberry
Robert Conrad
Marilyn Spores
Perry Fulkerson
Art Wiedinger
Kathleen Daly
Larry Rubin
Bob Bradley
Mark Bertolami
Tom Hawkins
Jack Whelan
*No Longer on Staff

RINGLING MUSEUM BOARD OF DIRECTORS

Chairman 2000 - present
Senator W. Marlow Cook, 2000 - 2001
Carolyn G. Johnson, 2001-2002
Vernon G. Buchanan, 2002 - 2004
Dorothy C. Jenkins, 2004 - 2005
Alice W. Rau, 2005 - present

Board of Directors
Sheila Austin-Smith*
Sara A. Bagley
David S. Band*
James S. Barnett*
Robert G. Blalock*
Vernon G. Buchanan
Robert E. Christopher
Senator Marlow W. Cook
Betty Doss*
Robert J. Geniesse
Arnold Greenfield*
Kay Culbreath Heller
Dorothy C. Jenkins
Christine L. Jennings
Carolyn G. Johnson
Senator Robert M. Johnson
Robert E. Koski
Beth K. Labasky*
G. Timothy Laney
Eleanor L. Merritt-Darlington
Senator John M. McKay
Simon Portnoy*
Alice W. Rau
Sandy Rief III
Robert G. Roskamp
T. Marshall Rousseau
John E. Sandefur

Barbara J. Siemer
Les R. Smout
David A. Straz, Jr.*
Howard C. Tibbals
Peter A. Vogt
Dr. Helga M. Wall-Apelt

Ex-Officio Board Members
Rhea Andrews*
Dorothy Brewer*
John B. Fisher
Allyn Gallup*
Sylvia Knight*
Richard R. Mottino
Barbara Sweeney*
Carolyn Ryan
*No Longer on Board

Ringling Museum Staff
Dr. John Wetenhall, Executive Director
Tess Koncick, Associate Director,
  Museum Collections & Programs
Chip Willis, Chief Operating Officer
Kathy Aberman
Charlyne Acree
Mina Ajrab
Jean Andrews
Ray Androne*
Connie Anglin
Kira Appel
Angie Apple
Michael Arch
Erica Bacon
Susan Barber
Lori Beier
Lynn Berkowitz
Loretta Bestpitch
Bill Booth

STAFF

Staff list as of Dec. 1, 2006

Angela Borges
Dr. Stephen Borys
Lynn Bourne-Weick*
Kathy Brooks
Tyrissa Bruss
Jill Burget
Frank Cantrell
Jennifer Carroll
Jay Cassidy
Jill Chamberlain*
Michael Chomick
Dr. Arland Christ-Janer*
Cindy Clenney (Vickers)
Jerry Clevenger*
Larry Conner
Melinda Cook
Hollie Corbitt
Fred Cornetta
Norman Cornwell
Ross Corona
Katrina Cromwell
Dwight Currie
Jelena Cvtkova
M. Noel DeBrick
Dr. Aaron DeGroft*
Karen Drake
Steve Dunay
Diana Easton
Dr. David Ebitz*
Ginny Eitman
Larissa Enzmann
Rick Esterly
Charles Fetherston*
Suellen Field
Charles Fish
Yadira Flores
Clarissa Fostel
Niki Garshelis*

James Gass
Cindy Gilligan
Buck Goggans
Beth Graves
Liz Gray
Kevin Greene
Francoise Hack
Gussie Haeffner
Cheryl Hagendorn
Matt Harmon
Jeanne Hendrick
Wally Herman
Lynn Hobeck Bates
Claude Hudon
Dick Inman
Joe Jackson
Carl Johnson
Loreen Kaser
Douglas Kingsley
Linda Kocourek*
Jennifer Kouvant*
Chrissy Kruger-Gruendyke
Mitch Ladewski
Jeanne Lambert*
Carl Lamparter
Arnold Larsen
Jennifer Lemmer Posey
Charles Lemon
Michele Leopold*
Lee Linkous, Jr.
Noel Lopez
Edward Mahieu
Ron Mallory
Martin Martinez
Michelle Maruca
Ron McCarty
Lyndsy McDonald
Linda McKee

Bill Mitchell
Jackie Moore
Frank Morton
Arron Muhl
Sandy Mytinger
George Naulty
Karen Newcomb
Cathy Orchowski
Marty Overstreet
Janine Packard
Bobbie Parks
Paula Parrish
Ed Parus
Joyce Peavey
Billy Pennington
Russ Pillifant
David Piurek
Melissa Porreca
Frank Quiming
Gary Ragan
Carlos Rivera
Donn Roll
Linda Romero
Derek Ross
Alan Rowley
Matt Rundell
Jennifer Sabo
Mark Sanderbeck
Jeff Santello
Michelle Scalera
Debi Schalch
Tracy Scharbach
Kate Schmitz
Bill Schwartz
Mark Sebzda
Selma Sellars
Debbie Serbousek
Virginia Shearer*

Rebecca Shields
Dan Simpler*
Lawrence Singer
Barbara Slater
Jeanie Speaker
Jon Tarro
Heidi Taylor
Carol Tayman
Peg Thornton
Laura Toney
Vinh Truyen
Lara Urfer
Debbie Walk
Susan Walker
Beth Wallace
Joanna Weber
Rebecca Wehr
Jerry Wendell
Howard Wheldon*
Artis Wick
Fred Wildt
Robert Wright
Maureen Zaremba
Robert Zimmermann
Marek Zmiejko

*No Longer on Staff

SPONSORS

Hellmuth, Obata + Kassabaum, Inc. (HOK), an international architectural firm with Florida offices in Tampa and Miami. Yann R. Weymouth, AIA, Director of Design and Senior Vice President of HOK, was in charge of the design for the Ringling's new Visitor Pavilion, the Gallery expansion and new Education Center.

Keith A. Millard Photography
Professional Photography Studio
2345 Bee Ridge Rd
Sarasota, FL 34239 USA
941-922-5911

Portrait – Events –Commercial

www.kamillard.com

 MASTER CONSULTING ENGINEERS, INC.

Master Consulting Engineers, Inc.,
www.mcengineers.com

PHOTOGRAPHY CREDITS

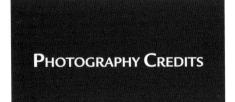

Keith A. Millard, pgs. Cover, IFC, 4, 10-11, 13, 18, 20-22, 24-27, 30-35, 39, 42, 45, 47, 58-59, 60, 64, 70
George Cott, pgs. Cover, 36-38, 39, 44, 46
Frank Atura, pgs. 5, 33, 50, IBC
HOK, pgs. 28-29, 70
Dick Dickinson, pgs. 48-49
Giovanni Lunardi pgs. Cover, 10, 12, 23, 25, 40, BC
Jim Stem, pgs. Cover, 55, 56
Herb Booth, pgs. 31, 52-53, 54
Other photos courtesy of The John and Mable Ringling Museum of Art.
All historic photographs found in the Museum Archives.

pg. 13 caption: Nicolas Poussin, French, 1594-1655, active in Rome and Paris
The Ecstasy of Saint Paul, 1643, Oil on Wood Panel, 16 $^{3/8}$ x 11 $^{7/8}$ inches.
Museum purchase, 1956, SN690